Do It Yourself

Paper Craft

Do It Yourself

Paper Craft

Author
Vinnie Mathur

Illustrator/ Design
Himani Pundir

Graphic Designer
Bhupender Singh

Galgotia Publications pvt. ltd.

Second Edition 2010

ISBN:- 81-7515-586-8

Published by Suneel Galgotia for Galgotia Publications Pvt. Ltd.,
5, Ansari Road, Darya Ganj, New Delhi-110 002 and
printed at :- Tara Art Printers Pvt. Ltd.

Galgotia Publications pvt. ltd.

CONTENTS

Ballerina Card 2
Bird Badges 4
Clown Face Mask 6
Chick Card 8
Gift Bag 10
Gift Box 12
Kite 14
Monster Mask 16
Paper Flowers 18
Paper Lantern 20
Paper Machie Fruit Bowl 23
Paper Pom Poms 25
Snowmen Card 27
Tiger Bookmark 29
Tweety Paper Album 31
Tissue Paper Card 33

Ballerina Card

Make this cute card for your friend on her birthday...

THINGS REQUIRED

- WHITE CARD
- PENCIL
- SKETCH PENS
- SCISSORS
- CRAFTY GLUE

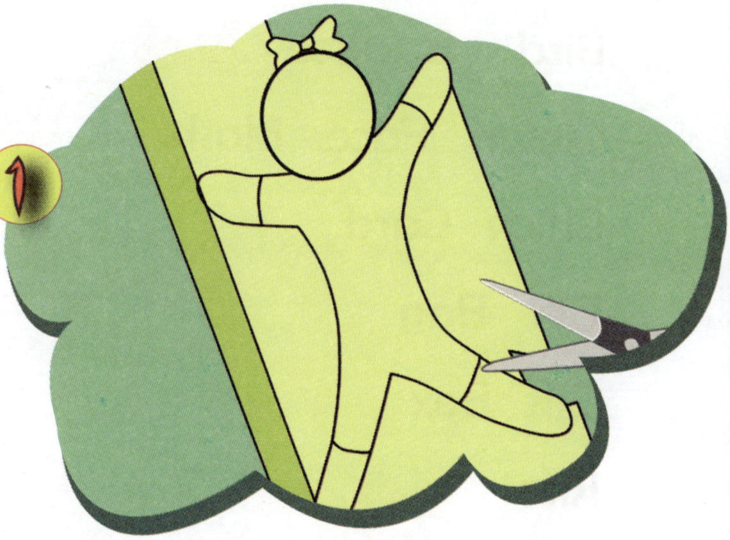

1

Draw a ballet dancer and cut her outline in three sheets so that you have cut outs of 3 dancers joined together.

2

Now colour the dancers in three different colours.

Write your message in the centre of the card.

Your ballerina card is ready now.

Bird Badges

THINGS REQUIRED

- OLD COPY COVER
- PAINTS & BRUSHES
- SAFTEY PINS
- SKETCH PENS
- DOUBLE TAPE

Take an old copy cover. Draw and cut out any shape of your choice like a fish or a bird etc. Alternately you can also cut out animals from magazine, old books etc.

Colour the bird shape, add its features with sketch pens.

Take a saftey pin and with a double tape, tape it at the back side. Your badge is now ready. Make more in different shapes and sizes.

Clown Face Mask

Make a clown face mask for yourself and your friend...

THINGS REQUIRED

- OLD COPY COVER
- PENCIL
- SCISSORS
- BLACK SKETCH PEN
- POSTER COLOURS
- THREAD

Draw the face of a clown on an old copy cover and cut it out.

Draw the outline with black sketch pen and punch two holes to make eyes.

3

Paint your clown using poster colours of your choice.

4

On the back side, attach a thread from one ear to the other ear.

Chick Card

Learn to make a simple pop up card...

Fold both the sheets of card in half. Cut a 6 cm slit in the white card at the centre of the folded sheet, at right angles to the fold.

Carefully fold in both the edges of the slit and make creases so that when you open and close the card, beak shape pops out.

Draw a large round chick's body around the beak shape. Use scribbly strokes to make the chick look fluffy.

Draw eyes and legs on the body with sketch pens. Cut the shape of wings from yellow paper and glue them to the body.

Your pop up chick card is ready.

Gift Bag

Let's learn to make a gift bag for presenting to your friends...

THINGS REQUIRED

- SHEET OF WRAPPING PAPER
- PENCIL
- RULER
- CRAFTY GLUE
- RIBBON

Take the wrapping paper and cut it into 45 x 30 cm size.

Draw two lines, 5 cms from the top and the bottom of the sheet. Then draw two lines of 20 cms from both the sides. Now fold and make creases.

Glue along the four long tabs as shown in the picture. Lift up the paper until edges X and Y meet. Press the long tabs together, then reach inside and pull up the small tabs, gluing them to the sides. You will have a box shape now.

Push the sides of the box together and make creases, so it looks like a bag. Punch two holes on each side at the top of the bag. Thread the ribbon through the outside holes on each side for making handles.

Lovely gift bag is ready. You can also make it with recycled paper.

Gift Box

Make this easy gift box and present sweets and chocolates to your friends and cousins...

THINGS REQUIRED

- THICK COLOURED PAPER 40X30 CMS
- SCISSORS
- RIBBON
- CRAFTY GLUE
- PUNCHING MACHINE

1

Take any coloured printed paper and fold into half.

2

Fold the paper again where they meet in the middle half line. Make sharp creases, then unfold the paper.

At 10 cms distance, make two marks. Fold the paper at the marks, then unfold. Cut three slits at the top and three at the bottom.

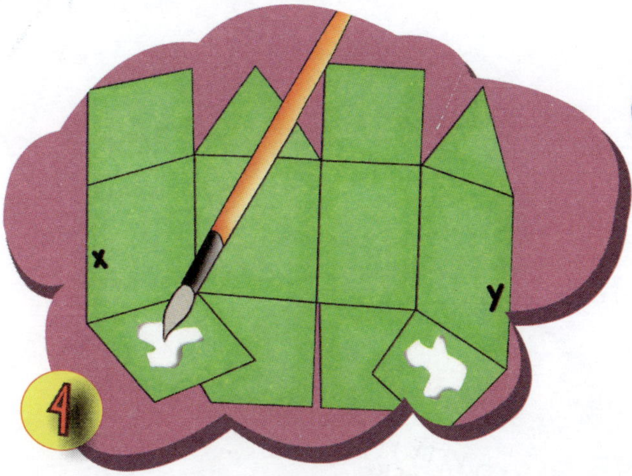

Cut the 2nd and 4th tabs into triangle shape. Put glue and shape the whole sheet into a box by bringing the edges X and Y together.

With the help of a punching machine, make a hole and thread the ribbon through the holes and tie a bow.

Kite

Let us learn how to make kites and be more creative and economical...

THINGS REQUIRED

- COLOURED KITE PAPER OR WRAPPING PAPER
- SCOTCH TAPE OR CRAFTY GLUE
- SCISSORS
- BROOM STICKS
- PAINTS, CRAYONS OR SPARKLES

Take a sheet of kite paper and cut a square from it.

Now take a stick out of a broom and paste it across the newspaper, using paper strips and glue or scotch tape as shown in the picture. Now the spine of the kite is ready.

Take another stick from the broom and bend it as shown in the picture. Paste the second stick in a curve shape on the earlier one.

Now make strips and stick at the end of the kite. Also add strips of coloured bunting to the end.

Your kite is now ready to fly.... You can decorate it further by colouring it in the colours of our national flag.

Monster Mask

THINGS REQUIRED

- SCRAP OF COLOURING PAPER FROM OLD BOOKS OR MAGAZINES
- A COLOURED SHEET OF PAPER
- CRAFTY GLUE
- SCISSORS
- ELASTIC

Draw the shape as shown on to the coloured sheet of paper and cut it out.

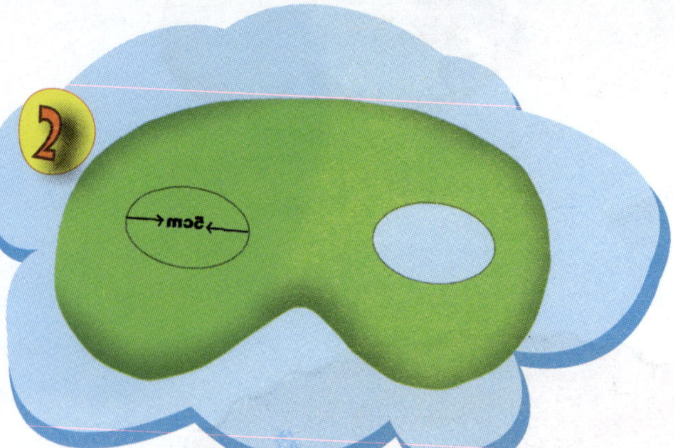

Cut out two eye holes in the mask about 5 cms apart.

Now cut out different shapes of paper in different colours and glue them on the back of the mask, around the edge.

4

Paste big black bindis for the eyes on to the front of the mask. Add coloured dots all over the mask. You can also use crushed foil to make small dots on the mask.

5

Make a small hole on each side and thread elastic through. Secure with knots. Your mask is ready.

Paper Flowers

Make these lovely pansies for presenting to your near and dear ones...

THINGS REQUIRED

- CREPE PAPER OF YELLOW AND GREEN COLOUR
- SCISSORS
- CRAFTY GLUE
- 2 PIECES OF WIRE
- BEADS
- BLACK FELT
- ZIG-ZAG SCISSORS

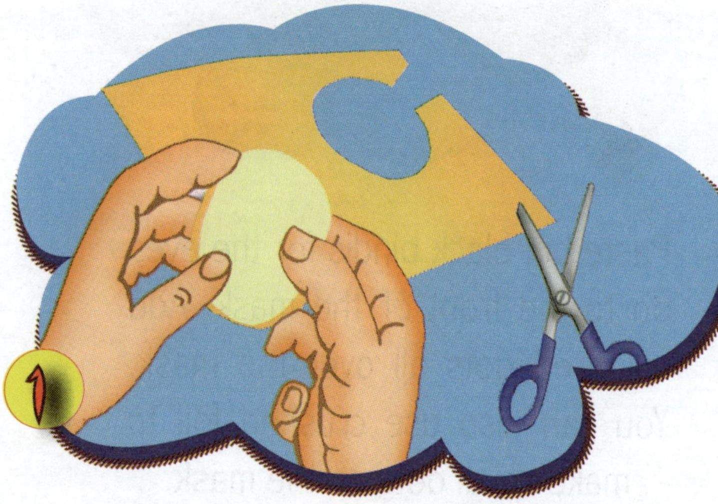

Cut out six circles from the yellow crepe paper, about 70 mm in diameter. Press them inside to make in a disc shape.

Thread the 20 black beads on to the wire. Twist the wire into a spiral shape.

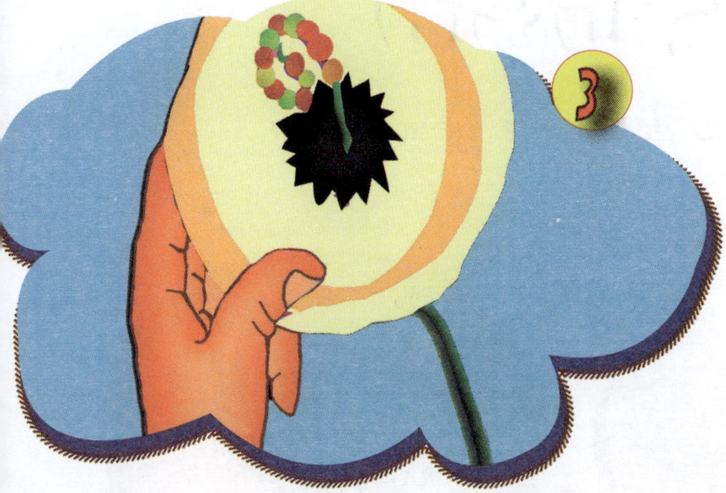

Now keep 6 paper discs on top of each other with the black felt small disc on top. Put the non-beaded end of the wire through the centre and pull it through.

To make the stem, take green crepe paper and glue around the wire spirally and your pansies are ready.

Let's say 'No to cut Flowers' and not to buy them from market, instead make on your own.

Paper Lantern

Make a paper lantern to decorate your room...

THINGS REQUIRED

- COLOURED PAPER
- CRAFTY GLUE
- PENCIL
- SCISSORS
- RULER
- SPARKLES

Draw vertical lines of 3 inches apart from each other as shown above.

Fold along the dotted lines and cut it.

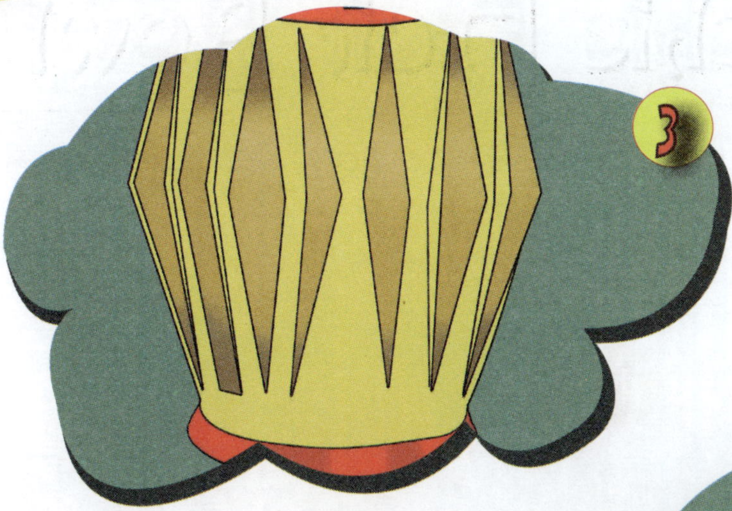

3

Open the paper strip and glue ends together.

4

Decorate the lantern with mirrors and sparkles. Add a strip of paper or ribbon rip of pape on top for it to hang.

Now you can hang the lantern in your room.

Paper Machie Fruit Bowl

Make this lovely fruit bowl to gift to your Granny...

THINGS REQUIRED

- NEWSPAPER STRIPS
- HAND BLENDER
- BUCKET
- ROUND BOWL
- OIL
- CRAFTY GLUE
- ACRYLIC COLOURS

Cut many strips out of newspaper.

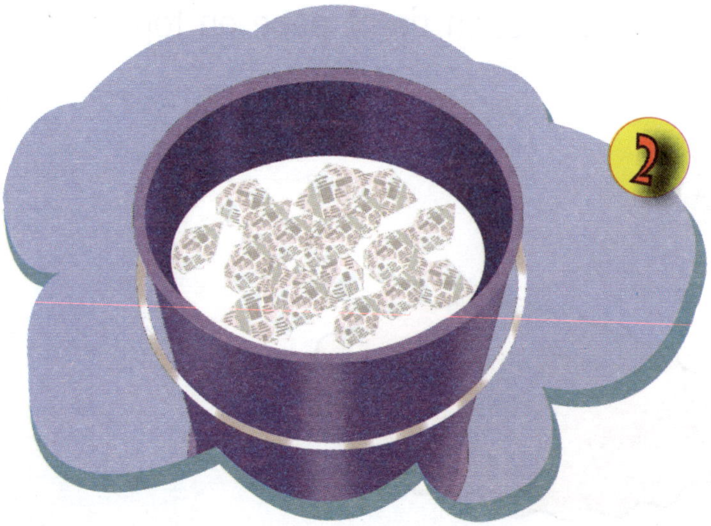

Soak the strips in a bucket of water overnight.

3

Change the water the next day and blend the mixture either in mixer or use a hand blender.

4

Mix 1 cup of pulp and half cup of glue together to make a smooth dough.

Now choose any bowl perferably big and spread it evenly in the shape of the bowl, using oil on your fingers. Now let it dry for 3-4 days. After it has dried take out the bowl.

Paint the fruit bowl with different acrylic colours and again let it dry for a day. Take a ribbon and tie it to both ends of the bowl to make a handle.

Eat fruits and be healthy and keep them in your own hand made fruit bowl.

Paper Pom-Poms

Make these lovely pom-poms to decorate your presents further...

THINGS REQUIRED

- COLOURED TISSUE PAPERS
- COLOURED PAPERS
- CRAFTY GLUE
- SCISSORS

1

Cut two strips of 40x12 cms from each sheet of tissue paper.

2

Put glue along the bottom edge of each strip and stick all four strips together.

3

Use scissors to snip along the strips, making each cut about 2 cms apart.

Spread glue along the bottom of the strip and roll the shape up. Press it together at the bottom and let it dry.

Now fluff it up with your fingers. Your pom-pom is ready. Make many more in different colours.

Decorate a special gift with these pom-poms.

Snowmen Card

Remain busy by making such cards for Xmas or New Year.

THINGS REQUIRED

- WHITE CARD
- PENCIL & RULER
- BLACK PAPER
- SKETCH PENS
- SLIVER GLITTER
- FEVICOL
- SCISSORS

Mark the card along the long side. Fold the card into three sections as shown in the picture above.

Draw a snowman shape on the card. Then cut out the shape, leaving it joined at the side.

Open up the card. Cut three hats from the black card and stick them on snowmen's heads.

Use sketch pen to draw eyes, mouth, buttons. Finish with orange carroty noses, walking sticks and scarfs. To further decorate, sprinkle some glitter for a sparkly touch.

Tiger Bookmark

Let the tiger help you read your favourite story...

THINGS REQUIRED

- ANY OLD GREETING CARD OR WEDDING CARD
- PENCIL
- SCISSORS
- CRAFTY GLUE
- GOOGLY EYES OR BINDIS
- BLACK SKETCH PEN

1

Draw an outline of a tiger face on paper and cut it out.

2

You can use the backside of an old greeting card or wedding card or use any colour paper of your choice. Cut it into the desired size of the bookmark.

Stick bindis or googly eyes and make its features like nose, whiskers, tongue etc.

When the face of the tiger is ready, stick it onto the cut long piece of thick paper.

Read your favourite book and use the bookmark.

Tweety Paper Album

Make this cute album to store your drawings, photographs and pictures...

Pile together six different sheets of card and punch two holes on one side.

THINGS REQUIRED

- 6 SHEETS OF COLOURED CARD
- SCRAPS OF COLOURED PAPER IN ANY 4 COLOURS
- RIBBON OF ANY COLOUR
- PUNCHING MACHINE
- ZIG-ZAG SCISSORS
- CRAFTY GLUE

Cut strips with zig-zag scissors from the scraps of coloured card. Arrange them to make a border on the cover and glue them.

Draw and cut a large tweety face and stick it on the cover. Now make its features like eyes, nose, eyebrows etc.

Thread the length of the ribbon through the holes, starting from the back including all the pages. Tie a bow at the front. Knot the ends of the ribbon to stop them from fraying.

Tweety album is ready. You can make different shapes like Noddy, Mickey Mouse etc.

Tissue Paper Card

Tissue papers are not only used to wipe hands but also to make beautiful cards. Let's see how...

THINGS REQUIRED

- SHEET OF WHITE CARD
- TISSUE PAPER IN RED, PINK, YELLOW
- CRAFTY GLUE
- PENCIL
- SPARKLES

1. Fold the card in half and run your finger firmly along the crease.

2. Fold the yellow tissue paper in half and lightly draw a heart shape next to the fold.

3. Tear the heart shape out of the tissue paper. Similarly make hearts of different sizes from the other sheets of tissue.

Carefully brush the glue onto the heart and stick them onto the card. Make the shape over-lap each other.

Roughly tear thin strips from the left over tissue and stick them around the edges of card to make a border. Further decorate by putting glitter or sparkles.

Your heart shaped card is ready.